Full STEAM Ahead!
Arts in Action

Creating Art Together

Robin Johnson

CRABTREE PUBLISHING COMPANY
WWW.CRABTREEBOOKS.COM

Title-Specific Learning Objectives:
Readers will:
- Identify different types of art and identify how the types can fit together.
- Explain that artists from different disciplines work together to create many kinds of art.
- Describe the connection between different artists, types of art, and parts of art.

High-frequency words (grade one)	Academic vocabulary
a, and, are, can, in, is, it, of, put, the, to	combine, creative, instruments, mural, perform, quilt, record, sculpture, skills, tools

Before, During, and After Reading Prompts:

Activate Prior Knowledge and Make Predictions:
Have children read the title and table of contents. Ask them what they think the book might be about. Encourage them to make text-to-self connections by asking questions such as:
- What does it mean to work together?
- Can you think of a time you worked with one or more people? How did working together help you?
- Why do you think artists might work together?

During Reading:
After reading pages 18 and 19, ask children:
- How do the different artists come together to make one piece of art?
- What words help you see the connection between the artists? Direct children to words such as together and another.

After Reading:
Have children work together to create a piece of art. Each group member must contribute something different to the art. Have children complete a verbal or written reflection that explains how it helped to work together with others to create the art.

Author: Robin Johnson
Series Development: Reagan Miller
Editor: Janine Deschenes
Proofreader: Melissa Boyce
STEAM Notes for Educators: Janine Deschenes
Guided Reading Leveling: Publishing Solutions Group
Cover, Interior Design, and Prepress: Samara Parent
Photo research: Robin Johnson and Samara Parent

Production coordinator: Katherine Berti

Photographs:
Alamy: Tuul and Bruno Morandi: p. 8; George Sweeney: p. 20
iStock: Lucy Brown - loca4motion: cover
Shutterstock: dmitro2009: p. 4; Igor Bulgarin: p. 9 (t); Goldquest: p. 9 (b); Art Babych: p. 10; Maljalen: p. 12; oki cahyo nugroho: p. 13 (t); windmoon: p. 13 (b); CHEN WS: p. 15 (b); Pavel L Photo and Video: p. 16; Mia2you: p. 18; Alina Reynbakh: p. 19 (t); eXpose: p. 19 (b)

All other photographs by Shutterstock

Library and Archives Canada Cataloguing in Publication
Title: Creating art together / Robin Johnson.
Names: Johnson, Robin (Robin R.), author.
Description: Series statement: Full STEAM ahead! | Includes index.
Identifiers: Canadiana (print) 20190133619 |
 Canadiana (ebook) 2019013366X |
 ISBN 9780778764601 (softcover) |
 ISBN 9780778764359 (hardcover) | ISBN 9781427123626 (HTML)
Subjects: LCSH: Artistic collaboration—Juvenile literature. |
 LCSH: Group work in art—Juvenile literature. |
 LCSH: Creation (Literary, artistic, etc.)—Juvenile literature.
Classification: LCC N7430.5 .J64 2019 | DDC j700—dc23

Library of Congress Cataloging-in-Publication Data
Names: Johnson, Robin (Robin R.), author.
Title: Creating art together / Robin Johnson.
Description: New York, New York : Crabtree Publishing Company, 2019. Series: Full STEAM ahead! | Includes index.
Identifiers: LCCN 2019026328 (print) | LCCN 2019026329 (ebook) |
 ISBN 9780778764359 (hardcover) |
 ISBN 9780778764601 (paperback) | ISBN 9781427123626 (ebook)
Subjects: LCSH: Artists--Juvenile literature. | Entertainers--Juvenile literature. | Cooperation--Juvenile literature.
Classification: LCC NX163 .J64 2019 (print) | LCC NX163 (ebook) | DDC 700.92--dc23
LC record available at https://lccn.loc.gov/2019026328
LC ebook record available at https://lccn.loc.gov/2019026329

Printed in the U.S.A./102019/CG20190809

Table of Contents

What is Art?.............. 4

Artists Have Skills 6

Working Together 8

Making Music.......... 10

Dance Partners........ 12

Showtime! 14

Helping to Create 16

Putting It All
Together 18

Sharing Art 20

Words to Know 22

Index and
About the Author.... 23

Crabtree Plus
Digital Code............ 23

STEAM Notes for
Educators................ 24

Crabtree Publishing Company
www.crabtreebooks.com 1-800-387-7650

Copyright © **2020 CRABTREE PUBLISHING COMPANY**. All rights reserved. No part of this publication may be reproduced, stored in a retrieval system or be transmitted in any form or by any means, electronic, mechanical, photocopying, recording, or otherwise, without the prior written permission of Crabtree Publishing Company. In Canada: We acknowledge the financial support of the Government of Canada through the Book Publishing Industry Development Program (BPIDP) for our publishing activities.

Published in Canada
Crabtree Publishing
616 Welland Ave.
St. Catharines, Ontario
L2M 5V6

Published in the United States
Crabtree Publishing
PMB 59051
350 Fifth Avenue, 59th Floor
New York, New York 10118

Published in the United Kingdom
Crabtree Publishing
Maritime House
Basin Road North, Hove
BN41 1WR

Published in Australia
Crabtree Publishing
Unit 3 – 5 Currumbin Court
Capalaba
QLD 4157

What is Art?

Art is all around us. It is anything made to be beautiful or interesting. It can be looked at and listened to. The people who make art are called artists.

Paintings are art we look at.

These people are dancing to music. Music and dance are both art.

These students are putting on a play. Their friends are watching them **perform**.

Artists Have Skills

Artists are **creative**. They have many ideas for new art. They also have skills. Artists learn their skills by practicing making art. Some artists learn skills at school too.

Artists make their ideas come to life. This paper art has a message inside. It says "good luck!"

Some artists teach skills to other artists.

These artists learned how to make art from wool.

Working Together

Artists can combine, or put together, their ideas and skills. They work together to make beautiful art!

Artists can work together to make pictures. Some pictures, such as this **mural**, are very big. Many artists worked together to paint it!

It takes days for these artists to make paintings out of sand. Working together helps them create art more quickly.

These artists are painting a colorful picture together.

Making Music

Artists can make music together. They use their voices to sing. They use instruments to make different sounds. The voices and sounds come together to make music.

These artists combine their voices to sing a song.

Instruments are tools that artists use to make music. Each instrument has a different sound. Artists blend the sounds together.

Dance Partners

Artists come together to dance in pairs or groups. They move their bodies to the sound of music. Together, they perform dances that people can watch.

These artists are dancing in pairs. They move their bodies together.

These artists do the same moves at the same time.

These artists are performing a **dragon dance**. Each dancer holds a piece of the dragon. They must work together to do their dance.

13

Showtime!

Artists work together to perform shows. They put on plays and puppet shows. They act in movies and TV shows.

Three artists work together to move this puppet.

These artists perform in a play. They work together to tell a story.

These artists perform tricks in a show. They work together to keep each other safe.

15

Helping to Create

It takes a lot of people to make shows! There are many artists we do not see. Artists write stories. They build **sets**. They make costumes and do makeup.

These artists are using tools such as cameras and lights to make a movie.

This artist is putting makeup on an actor.

This artist is making costumes for a TV show.

17

Putting It All Together

Artists have different skills. They make different types of art. They can put their art together to make something special.

Artists put **sculptures** and paintings together to make this art display.

This dancer is an artist. Another artist made her dress. A third artist makes the music she dances to. They put their art together to make one beautiful dance.

An artist designed this interesting building. Another artist added colorful lights to make it shine at night.

Sharing Art

Artists can work together even when they are far apart. They create art where they live. Then they share it with other artists around the world.

It took hundreds of artists to make this huge **quilt**. People around the world sent patches to help make it.

Artists from different places can work together to make music. They each record their part. Then, an artist puts all the parts together to make a song.

This artist is drawing a flower on a computer. She will share it with other artists to make a book.

Words to Know

creative [kree-EY-tive] adjective Able to imagine and create new things

dragon dance [DRAG-uh n dans] noun A traditional Chinese dance, often performed at celebrations

mural [MYOOR-uh l] noun A large picture painted directly on a wall

perform [per-FAWRM] verb To put on a show for people to watch

quilt [kwilt] noun A blanket made of patches

sculptures [SKUHLP-chers] noun Art made by shaping and putting together materials

set [set] noun A human-made setting, or place, used for a scene in a play, movie, or TV show

---

A noun is a person, place, or thing.
A verb is an action word that tells you what someone or something does.
An adjective is a word that tells you what something is like.

Index

computer 21
costume 16–17
dance 5, 12–13, 19
dragon dance 13
instruments 10–11
makeup 16–17

mural 8
music 5, 10–11, 19, 21
painting 4, 8–9, 18
perform 5, 12–13, 14–15
play 5, 14–15
set 16

About the Author

Robin Johnson is a freelance author and editor who has written more than 80 children's books. When she isn't working, Robin builds castles in the sky with her engineer husband and their two best creations—sons Jeremy and Drew.

To explore and learn more, enter the code at the Crabtree Plus website below.

www.crabtreeplus.com/fullsteamahead

Your code is:
fsa20

STEAM Notes for Educators

Full STEAM Ahead is a literacy series that helps readers build vocabulary, fluency, and comprehension while learning about big ideas in STEAM subjects. *Creating Art Together* introduces readers to connections within a text, as they explore how different artists, types of art, and parts of art are connected. The STEAM activity below helps readers extend the ideas in the book to build their skills in arts and science.

Collaborative Art Display

Children will be able to:
- Collaborate to put together three different types of art in one art display.
- Create an art display that represents a science concept learned in class.

Materials
- Art materials and tools, including sponges, craft sticks, paper, rulers, tape, glue, brushes, feathers, paint, clay, pencils, crayons, stones, petals, plastic blocks or toys, canvas, etc.
- Art Display Planning Sheet

Guiding Prompts
After reading *Creating Art Together*, ask children to consider why collaboration is important. Encourage them to use evidence from the book to support their ideas. Ask questions such as:
- Why do artists work together?
- Can you name some examples from this book that show how artists worked together?
- Why is working together useful?

Activity Prompts
Review the image on page 18, which shows an art display. Ensure that children understand what this kind of art display is—a collection that shows visual art. Many artists collaborated to put different kinds of art together in this display. Explain to children that they will create their own art displays! Each child collaborates with two peers. Each group of three needs to create an art display with three different kinds of art. The educator may choose to review kinds of art, such as paintings, drawings, sculptures, mosaics, etc.

Each display must include art that represents, or stands for, an idea in a science unit. Educator can integrate this activity with any chosen science unit. For example, children could create art related to weather, living things, or forces.

Hand each group an Art Display Planning Sheet. Then, give groups time to create their art displays. Have groups set up their displays and explain how their art represents science ideas.

Extensions
- Invite children to use technology to photograph or record a video of their art displays, then post on a class web page.

To view and download the worksheet, visit **www.crabtreebooks.com/resources/printables** or **www.crabtreeplus.com/fullsteamahead** and enter the code **fsa20**.